SUPERCAR

Editorial:	Steve Parker
Design:	David West
	Children's Book Design
Illustrator:	Ron Hayward
Picture research:	Cecilia Weston-Baker
Consultant:	Christopher Willows, BMW (GB) Ltd

© Aladdin Books Ltd 1988

Created and designed by
N. W. Books Ltd
70 Old Compton Street
London W1

First published in the
United States in 1988 by
Gloucester Press
387 Park Avenue South
New York, NY 10016

ISBN 0-531-17098-5

Library of Congress Catalog
Card Number: 88-50516

Contents

ENGINEERS AT WORK

SUPERCAR

MIKE TRIER

GLOUCESTER PRESS

New York · London · Toronto · Sydney

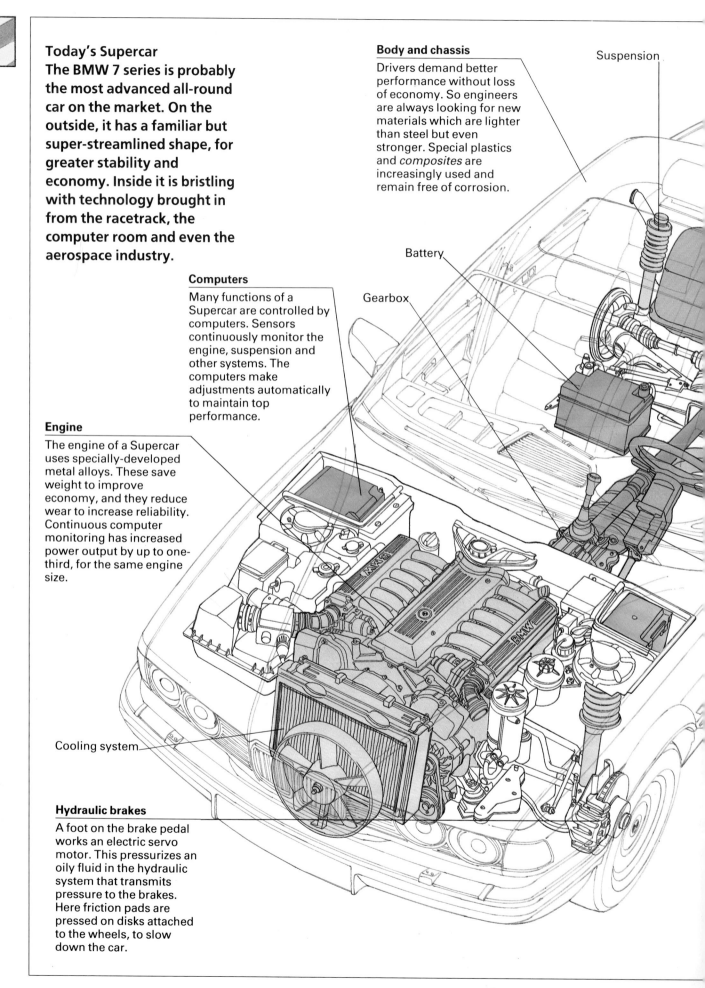

Today's Supercar
The BMW 7 series is probably the most advanced all-round car on the market. On the outside, it has a familiar but super-streamlined shape, for greater stability and economy. Inside it is bristling with technology brought in from the racetrack, the computer room and even the aerospace industry.

Body and chassis
Drivers demand better performance without loss of economy. So engineers are always looking for new materials which are lighter than steel but even stronger. Special plastics and *composites* are increasingly used and remain free of corrosion.

Suspension

Battery

Gearbox

Computers
Many functions of a Supercar are controlled by computers. Sensors continuously monitor the engine, suspension and other systems. The computers make adjustments automatically to maintain top performance.

Engine
The engine of a Supercar uses specially-developed metal alloys. These save weight to improve economy, and they reduce wear to increase reliability. Continuous computer monitoring has increased power output by up to one-third, for the same engine size.

Cooling system

Hydraulic brakes
A foot on the brake pedal works an electric servo motor. This pressurizes an oily fluid in the hydraulic system that transmits pressure to the brakes. Here friction pads are pressed on disks attached to the wheels, to slow down the car.

SUPERCAR!

In our modern world, engineering and technology are becoming more and more complex. Researchers develop new metals, plastics and other materials. Computers are used in design and the finished product. Customers demand increased safety and lower running costs, yet they also want extra performance and more reliability. Manufacturers must keep ahead of competitors.

At the center of design and production are the engineers. Their work today will solve the problems posed by tomorrow's structures and machines, from skyscrapers to bridges, oil rigs, airliners – and cars. The car is essential to today's way of life, but it has faults. It pollutes the air and it uses up natural resources (such as petroleum that gas is made from). Its roadways scar the land, and people die in road accidents. The engineer's job is to increase safety, performance and reliability. Today's Supercars are the super-sedans, technically the most advanced all-round cars on the market. They can be used to take children to school or tour non-stop across a continent. They show the way to cars of the future.

A body shaped for the job
Different types of car fulfill various roles. A family sedan must seat four or five people in comfort and still have room for luggage. The hatchback can be converted to carry larger loads. A sports car is low and sleek. An economy sedan must handle well in traffic.

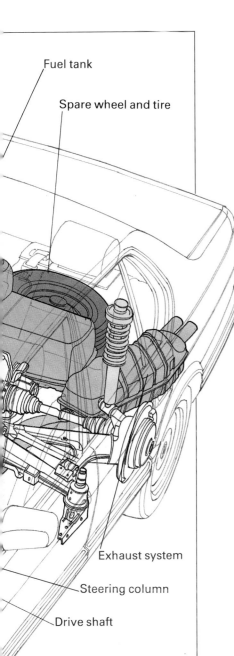

Fuel tank

Spare wheel and tire

Exhaust system

Steering column

Drive shaft

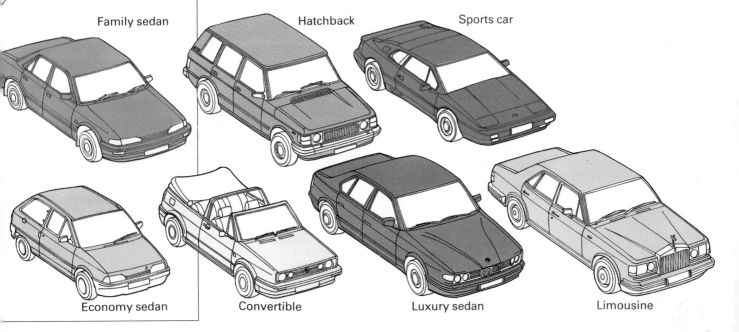

Family sedan

Hatchback

Sports car

Economy sedan

Convertible

Luxury sedan

Limousine

CONCEPT AND DESIGN

The first problem in producing a new car is: where do you start? Designers may be asked to restyle an existing model or produce a completely new car. Restyling may work for some types of car, but for a Supercar there is only one answer: start from scratch, so that new technologies and techniques can be used to the full. However, it's not quite like an artist beginning work on a blank canvas. There are restrictions. Countries have various

Wind tunnel testing
Tests are made on a very accurate model of the car, in clay, plaster or fiberglass. Then adjustments to the shape can be made before production begins. Giant fans blow air past the model at up to 200 km/h (125 mph). Smoke jets show the direction of flow.

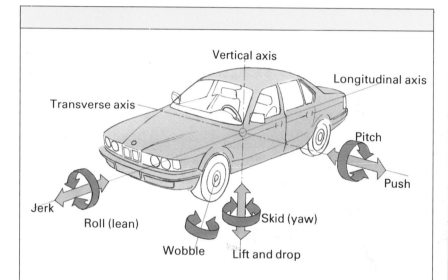

Vertical axis
Longitudinal axis
Transverse axis
Pitch
Push
Jerk
Roll (lean)
Skid (yaw)
Wobble
Lift and drop

FORCES ON THE FRAME

The diagram shows the stresses on a moving car. Computer simulation shows how much stress must be absorbed to keep the wheels in contact with the road. In the BMW 7, CAD (Computer-Aided Design) helped to develop a rigid but efficient body shape.

regulations, such as the height of the bumper from the ground, or the amount any part (like an outside mirror) can project from the general body shape. There are technical considerations, too. Will it be possible to form metal and plastic to the curves the designer wants? And there are automobile "fashions" – will customers like the look of the car?

Car designers are always trying to lower the *drag coefficient*. This means they streamline the body to reduce wind resistance – but still keep space inside so that people are comfortable. Streamlining enables the car to go faster, and improves road-holding and fuel economy.

MODEL CARS

To test the Supercar's shape an accurate model is made. The design is drawn by an artist (1). When the general shape is agreed, scale models are made in plaster or clay (2), to work out the detailed outlines. Then the final version is constructed (3), and the designers can see how it looks.

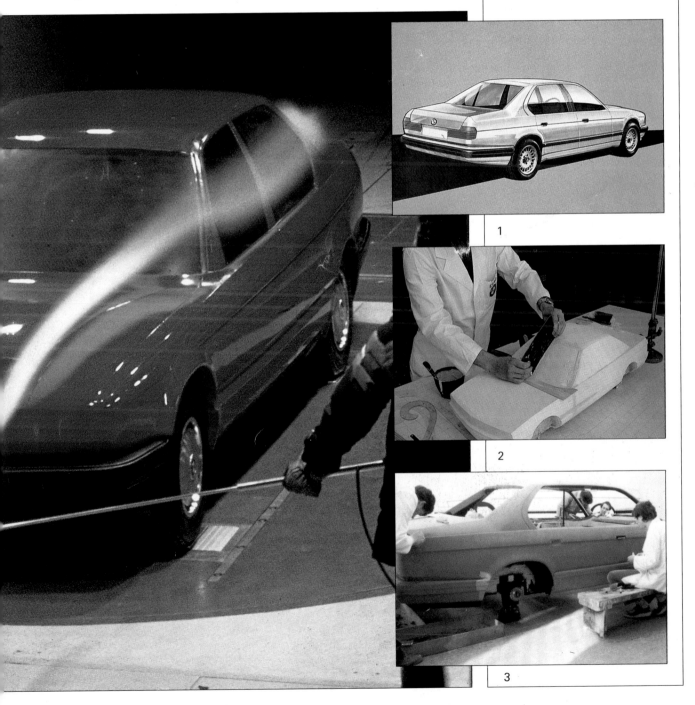

1

2

3

POWER IN THE MACHINE

The engine is the heart of the car. For a new model, the manufacturer has the choice of using an existing and well-proven engine – or developing a new one, which could be used in future models. For a Supercar, the only real option is to develop a brand-new engine using the latest engineering techniques. Problems are considerable. A Supercar must show good performance and economy, both in city traffic and on long-haul trips. It

Computer management

A computer system improves engine efficiency by monitoring performance using sensors. As well as fuel injection, computer circuits control ignition timing (the moment at which the spark plugs fire) and check the purity of the exhaust.

Fuel injection

In advanced engines, fuel is pushed or "injected" into the cylinder, rather than simply being sucked in. This gives more power. A sensor detects the amount of air being drawn into the engine. It sends a signal to an electronic control unit. This opens the fuel injection valve long enough to produce the optimum mixture of fuel and air in the cylinder. This happens many times each second!

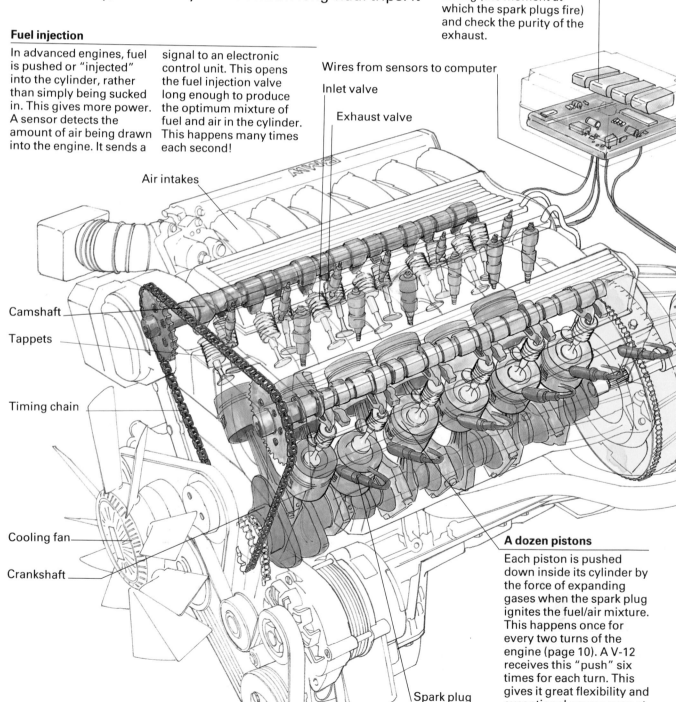

Wires from sensors to computer

Inlet valve

Exhaust valve

Air intakes

Camshaft

Tappets

Timing chain

Cooling fan

Crankshaft

Spark plug

A dozen pistons

Each piston is pushed down inside its cylinder by the force of expanding gases when the spark plug ignites the fuel/air mixture. This happens once for every two turns of the engine (page 10). A V-12 receives this "push" six times for each turn. This gives it great flexibility and exceptional power even at low speeds.

should glide like a limousine, yet accelerate like a sports car.

The Supercar's engine is not thrown together in an oily workshop. It is a precision machine, assembled in controlled, dust-free surroundings. Specialist parts such as temperature-resistant alloys are supplied by a number of manufacturers. Quality control is vital, to ensure that all parts fit together exactly. Rigorous testing is also essential, to make sure that components do not fail under the enormous stresses inside an engine turning at 7,000 revolutions each minute. Friction is one of the engineer's greatest problems. Efficient cooling and lubrication systems must keep wear and tear to a minimum.

The V-12 engine
The BMW 750's V-12 engine combines enormous power with great smoothness. V-12 means the engine has 12 cylinders, arranged in two banks (rows) of 6, with the two banks set at a V-shaped angle to each other. Each bank may be fueled independently so that, if one fails, the other still runs.

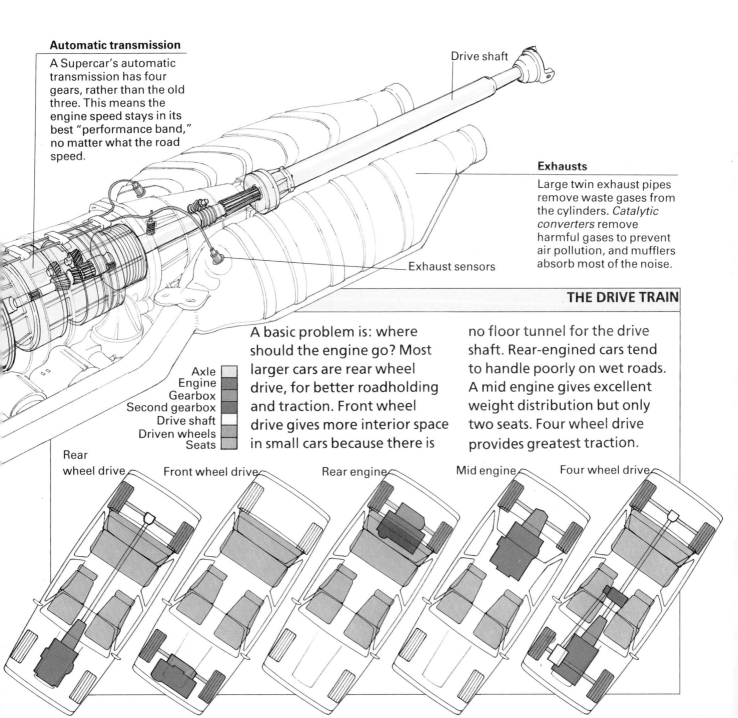

Automatic transmission
A Supercar's automatic transmission has four gears, rather than the old three. This means the engine speed stays in its best "performance band," no matter what the road speed.

Drive shaft

Exhausts
Large twin exhaust pipes remove waste gases from the cylinders. *Catalytic converters* remove harmful gases to prevent air pollution, and mufflers absorb most of the noise.

Exhaust sensors

THE DRIVE TRAIN

Axle
Engine
Gearbox
Second gearbox
Drive shaft
Driven wheels
Seats

A basic problem is: where should the engine go? Most larger cars are rear wheel drive, for better roadholding and traction. Front wheel drive gives more interior space in small cars because there is no floor tunnel for the drive shaft. Rear-engined cars tend to handle poorly on wet roads. A mid engine gives excellent weight distribution but only two seats. Four wheel drive provides greatest traction.

Rear wheel drive

Front wheel drive

Rear engine

Mid engine

Four wheel drive

The intelligent engine

The computer is the "brain" behind the Supercar's engine. It keeps track of dozens of functions and adjusts them continuously, to keep the engine performing at its best.

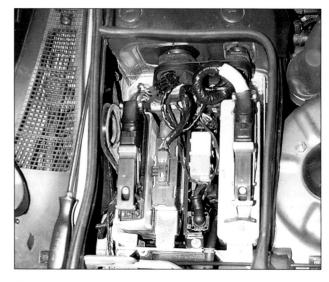

Engine management

The engine computer receives thousands of signals each second from sensors in various parts of the car. Every microsecond, as the car speeds up, slows down, or goes uphill or down, it decides which adjustments are needed for efficient engine operation. It then sends out signals to make those adjustments. In addition to reacting to signals from the airflow, throttle, engine speed and exhaust sensors, it may be linked to the anti-lock braking system. This limits acceleration and so prevents wheel spin.

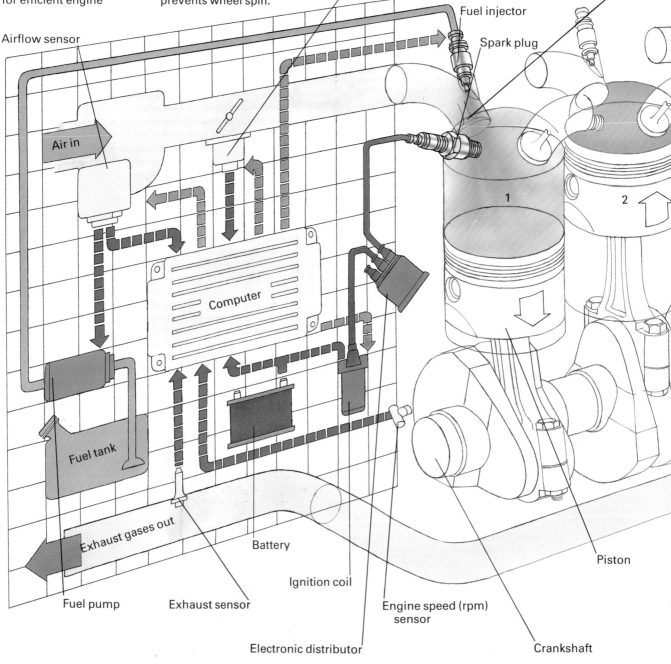

Throttle (accelerator) sensor

Inlet valve opens

Fuel injector

Spark plug

Airflow sensor

Air in

Computer

1

2

Fuel tank

Exhaust gases out

Battery

Piston

Fuel pump

Exhaust sensor

Ignition coil

Engine speed (rpm) sensor

Electronic distributor

Crankshaft

Four-stroke cycle

All modern engines use this cycle, shown from left to right. (1) Induction: fuel/air mixture is drawn into cylinder. (2) Compression: mixture is squeezed. (3) Ignition: spark plug fires to explode mixture, forcing piston downward. (4) Exhaust: hot exhaust gases are swept out of cylinder.

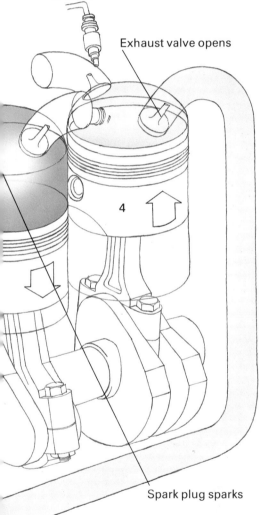

Exhaust valve opens

4

Spark plug sparks

In today's competitive market, engineers must decide how to boost the power of an engine without losing economy. This often means developing new technology. An engine can be made more powerful by giving it more cylinders, or by making each cylinder bigger. But this makes the engine heavier, so some of the advantage is lost. Also, there are mechanical limits on how big a cylinder can be. Supercars take advantage of computer management, as shown on the left, to increase the efficiency of the engine.

Turbochargers are now used on some cars to increase power and efficiency. Normally, exhaust gases go to waste. A "turbo" uses these fast-moving gases to spin a turbine (a special fan). This drives a compressor which forces air into the engine, much like fuel is "injected." The system improves fuel combustion. Increasing the number of valves per cylinder from two to four also helps. It allows the fuel/air mixture to change more quickly and thoroughly, so extracting every ounce of power.

State-of-the-art

Cosworth's 16-V Turbo has four valves per cylinder, overhead camshafts and turbocharging. It produces almost twice the power of the standard 2-litre, 4-cylinder Ford engine on which it is based.

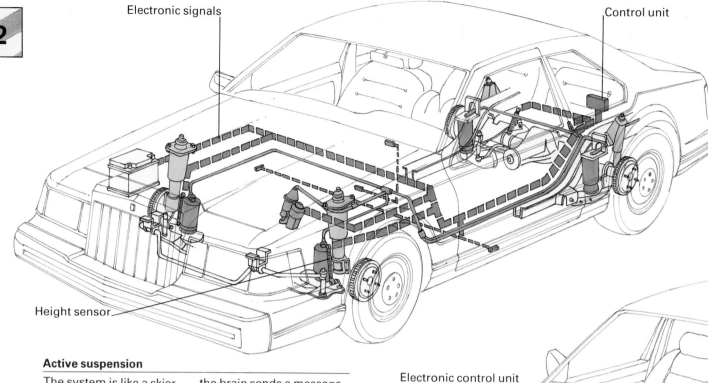

Electronic signals

Control unit

Height sensor

Active suspension

The system is like a skier racing downhill. The nerves in the skier's feet are height sensors, his brain the control module, and his leg muscles the suspension. When the skier passes over a bump, the nerves in his feet send a message to his brain saying that the feet have moved upwards. Instantly, the brain sends a message back along nerves to his leg muscles, which shorten to bend his legs, so that his body remains steady. In the same way the control module sends electronic signals to adjust the suspension and keep the car level, as it corners and passes over bumps and holes in the road.

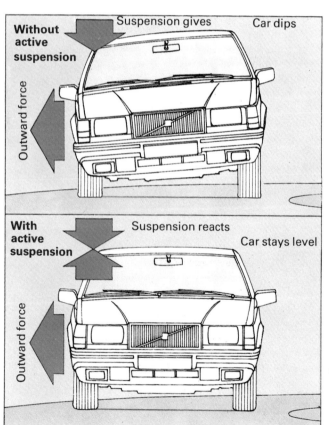

Suspension gives   Car dips

Without active suspension

Outward force

With active suspension

Suspension reacts   Car stays level

Outward force

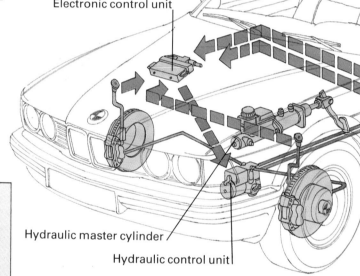

Electronic control unit

Hydraulic master cylinder

Hydraulic control unit

Anti-lock brake system (ABS)

In the ABS system, wheel sensors detect how fast each wheel rotates. If a driver stamps on the brake pedal, the brakes may "lock" the wheels (stop them rotating suddenly), leading to a skid and poor braking. When a wheel is about to lock, the control unit tells the hydraulic unit to reduce the brake pressure on that wheel. This gives smooth braking.

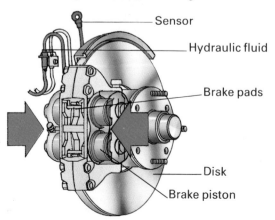

Sensor

Hydraulic fluid

Brake pads

Disk

Brake piston

STEERING AND STOPPING

The steering, suspension and brakes have great effect on the performance, handling and safety of a car. Conventional suspension, using springs and shock absorbers, has been in use for many years. It helps to smooth out bumps and holes in the road, but still transmits some movements to the car body. How could it be improved? One answer is *active suspension*. A control module assesses almost instantly what is happening at each suspension point, and takes action before any movement of the car body occurs.

Computerized anti-lock braking systems are another great advance. They reduce braking distances by as much as 40 per cent on wet roads. Electronic power-assisted steering also makes driving easier. It give greatest help to the driver at low speeds and during parking, when it is normally hardest to turn the steering wheel. Power assistance is less at high speeds, when it is easier to turn the wheel. This keeps a positive "feel" to the steering.

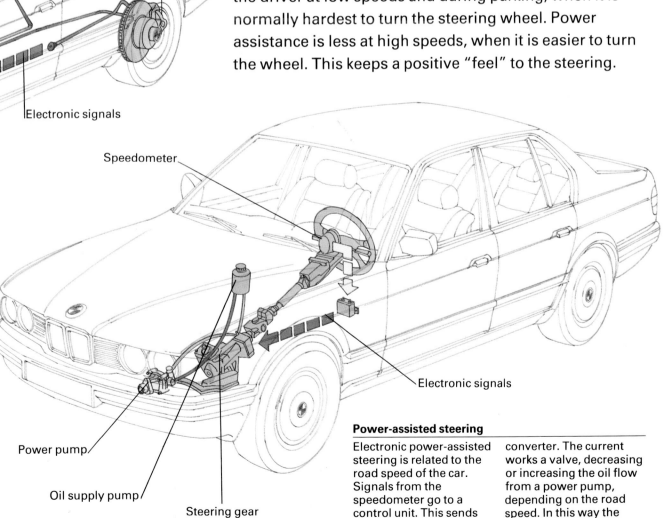

Disk brake

Electronic signals

Speedometer

Electronic signals

Power pump

Oil supply pump

Steering gear
Electric/hydraulic
converter

Power-assisted steering

Electronic power-assisted steering is related to the road speed of the car. Signals from the speedometer go to a control unit. This sends electric signals to the electric/hydraulic converter. The current works a valve, decreasing or increasing the oil flow from a power pump, depending on the road speed. In this way the degree of power assistance is changed.

COMPUTER-CAR!

Electronics play an increasing role in Supercars. The more elaborate the car, the more electronics are used to control the various functions. There is also a trend to move away from often troublesome mechanical linkages, with their wear and tear problems. Instead, an electronic sensor is used to control an electric motor or valve, the two being connected by wires. It might seem that this would greatly increase the number of electrical parts. But computer technology means that engineers can fit thousands of circuits onto one silicon chip the size of a fingernail.

In addition to controlling performance, electronics can also detect problems. These can then be displayed on the dashboard, in order of priority, for the driver. Also, a record of the car's problems is stored in a computer memory. When the car is in need of servicing, it can be plugged into the servicing computer. This gives a printout of any repairs needed. For export, when a different language is needed on the dashboard display – simply change the chip!

Computer power galore

An advanced Supercar such as the BMW 7 has a number of "computers" spread around the car. If one develops a fault, the others should not be affected – in fact they can take over some functions. The crash sensor detects when there has been an accident, and automatically releases the electronically-locked doors so that the people can escape. When the car is put into reverse gear, the outside mirror automatically tilts down slightly so that the driver can see the ground and curb behind clearly. Each function is designed for safer, more comfortable driving.

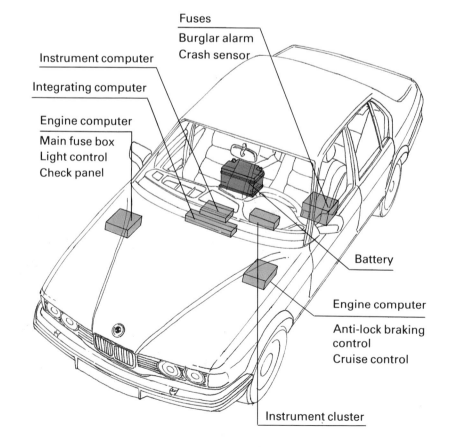

Fuses
Burglar alarm
Crash sensor

Instrument computer

Integrating computer

Engine computer
Main fuse box
Light control
Check panel

Battery

Engine computer

Anti-lock braking control
Cruise control

Instrument cluster

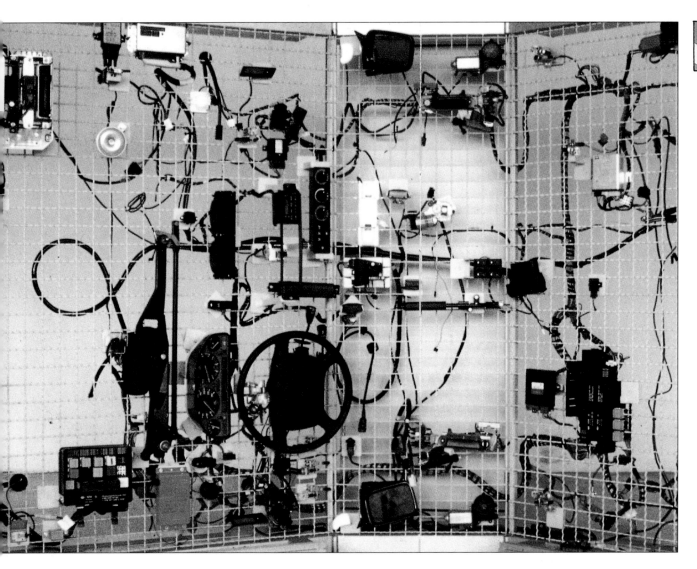

International Supercar

The set-up above shows a BMW 7's electrical and computer systems strung out on a grid, in the form of a real-life diagram. Main trunking cables enclose many smaller wires and carry them from one area to another. On the right, today's car market is truly international. Messages that may flash on the readout display next to the main instrument cluster can be in German, English or French.

German	English	French
Check-Control	CHECK CONTROL	CHECK-CONTROLE
Handbremse lösen	PARKING BRAKE ON	OTER FREIN MAIN
Bremsflüssigkeit	LOW BRAKE FLUID	LIQUIDE FREINS
Bremsdruck	BRAKE PRESSURE	PRESSION FREINS
Oelstand Motor	ENGINE OIL LOW	NIV.HUILE MOTEUR
Oelst.Lenkhilfe	POW STEER FLUID	NIV.HUILE DIRECT
Waschwasserstand	WASHER FLUID LOW	NIV. LAVE-GLACES
Licht?	LIGHT ON?	ECLAIRAGE MIS?
Abblendlicht	LOW BEAM	FEUX CROISEMENT
Nebellicht hint.	R/FOG LIGHT	FEUX BROUILL AR
Bremslicht	BRAKE LIGHT	FEUX STOP
Schiebedach off.	SUNROOF OPEN	TOIT OUVR.OUVERT
Fenster offen	WINDOW OPEN	VITRE OUVERTE
Tür offen	DOOR OPEN	PORTE OUVERTE

INSIDE A SUPERCAR

One problem for the designers of a car is that people come in various shapes and sizes. The driving seat must be adjustable so that a tall person and a short one feel equally comfortable. Are all the main controls naturally at hand? Is the instrument display clearly visible without having to move the head too much? And is there good all-round visibility for the driver, without having so much glass that the car is like a hothouse in summer? Will noise from the engine, wind and road be kept out? Each problem must receive full consideration. People-shaped "cutouts" help the designers to produce working drawings of the interior. A "seat box" (a full-scale model of the interior) enables the designers and engineers to test *ergonomics* – the ease of reading and operating all the instruments, controls and fittings.

Great attention is also paid to safety. There must be no hard or sharp areas inside which could cause injury. Seat belts must be anchored at the correct height and hold the occupants without restriction. Their effectiveness has to be proved in crash tests.

See-through wheel

The driver has a clear view of the instruments through the steering wheel and easy access to the control stalks. In some models an airbag is built into the steering column. This automatically inflates in the event of a frontal collision, to prevent head and chest injuries.

Seats

Both front seats are electrically adjustable. The computer memorizes the positions for a number of drivers. Press a button and it adjusts the seat, together with the height of the seat belt points and the position of the outside mirrors.

Ventilation

Vents are fitted in the front and rear of the car, and the driver and front passenger have independent controls. The system gives comfort from the Arctic to the Sahara.

Sounds of silence

A Supercar must be quiet inside, even at high speeds, and quiet on the outside, too. A special sound room (below) lets engineers measure sound levels. Hinged plastic models of people (far right) help the designers to make working drawings of the car's interior.

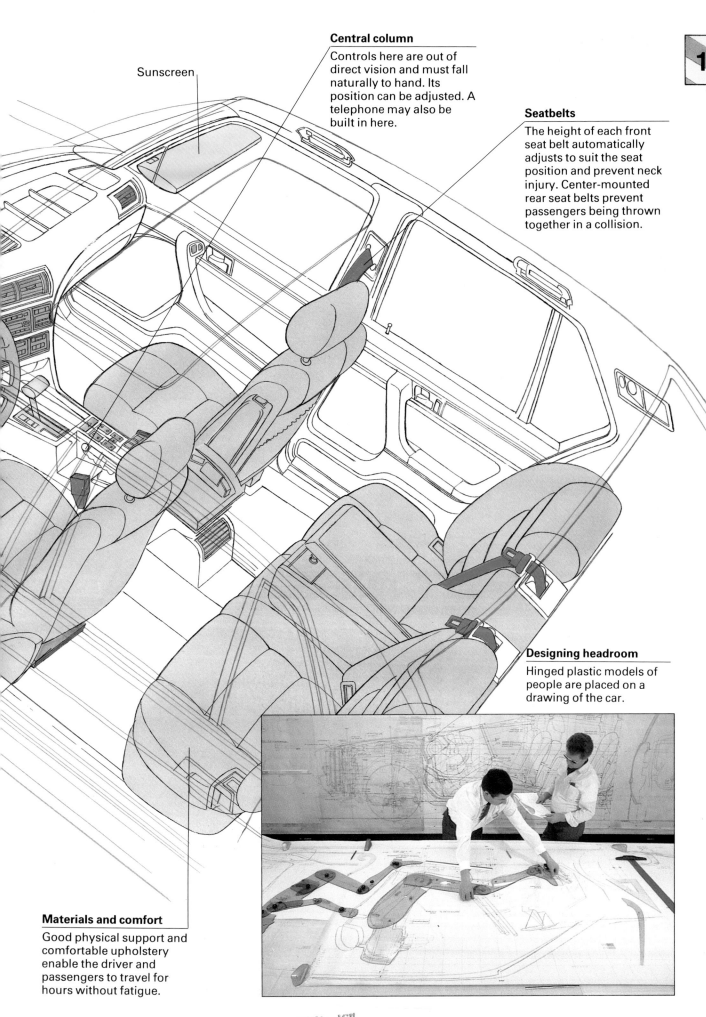

Sunscreen

Central column

Controls here are out of direct vision and must fall naturally to hand. Its position can be adjusted. A telephone may also be built in here.

Seatbelts

The height of each front seat belt automatically adjusts to suit the seat position and prevent neck injury. Center-mounted rear seat belts prevent passengers being thrown together in a collision.

Designing headroom

Hinged plastic models of people are placed on a drawing of the car.

Materials and comfort

Good physical support and comfortable upholstery enable the driver and passengers to travel for hours without fatigue.

BUILDING PROTOTYPES

Developing a Supercar is enormously expensive. Thorough testing is essential to remove problems before the production line is set up and the model is launched on the market. To do this, prototypes are built. These are fully working cars, each one made individually by engineers and craftsmen. For the BMW 7 Supercar, 400 cars were hand-built on the factory production line, to test both the car itself and the manufacturing techniques. The most advanced measuring technology was needed, because the prototypes were used as the basis for making the production-line machinery and tools. Each car took weeks to construct, ensuring it would withstand the extensive testing program both on and off the road.

At each stage, mechanical parts were checked for wear and tear, to make sure they were not loose or near to breaking point. The position of some components, such as cables, was best found by trial and error. Because of today's competitive car market, the manufacturers decided to disguise their new cars during road tests. This meant their competitors learned as little as possible!

THE PARTS MAKE THE WHOLE

Developing a Supercar requires teams of designers and engineers. Each team concentrates on a particular system or structure, such as the body shell or suspension. Detailed drawings are produced during the prototype stage. Eventually the finalized drawings are sent out to the many factories which subcontract the making of specialist components. Engineers keep a close watch on standards of workmanship, materials and accuracy, so that the parts fit together properly on assembly.

Hand-built
Prototypes are constructed entirely by hand, ironing out problems along the way.

Is it, isn't it . . ?
Two prototypes sit in a street, disguised so as to avoid unwanted attention.

Electrical parts
Advanced electronic monitoring has pushed up the number of electrical components, but these are generally small, light and reliable. A BMW 7 has 5,000 feet of wiring!

Body
Besides the main shell, there are shaped components of plastic and textiles, and special weight-saving composites. Total number of parts is about 600.

How many components?
Today's Supercar is an intricate assembly of some 20,000 parts, from the main body shell to tiny rubber seals and plastic screws. For each and every part there are questions for the engineer. What should it be made of? Is it the optimum shape? Can we save on weight? Is it strong enough? Will it last? And what will happen if it fails?

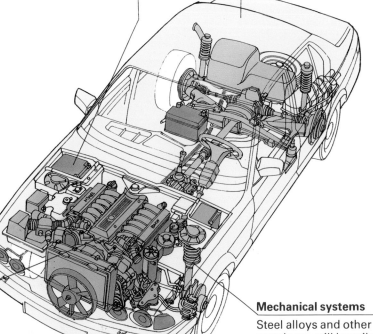

Engine
Many engine parts are now made of lightweight alloys that resist wear, lubricate well, and do not deform at high temperatures.

Mechanical systems
Steel alloys and other metals are still heavily used for steering, suspension, brakes and other highly stressed systems.

ON TRIAL

Once the prototypes are completed, tests begin. These fall into two main types: simulated tests and road tests.

The most important advantage of simulated tests is that they are carried out under controlled "laboratory" conditions, unaffected by the surroundings. So they can be repeated exactly, many times. The engineers use computerized testing programs. They select the sequence of events, record and sort the information from the test, and assess the results. For example, a simulated drive through a town can be carried out on a "rolling road" – without the car moving an inch. Engineers collect and analyze exhaust gases, to check pollution levels and engine performance.

Road testing is carried out both on a test track and on public roads. Computer monitoring equipment sits in the passenger seat, making the interior of the car look like a recording studio – which is more or less what it is! The test track includes water splashes, to check that the bodywork does not leak and the electrical circuits are waterproof.

Artificial winter

In the engineer's research workshops, temperatures can be taken down to minus 40°C. This simulates the coldest winters the car is likely to encounter. When engineers go into the room they must wear special Eskimo-style padded coats, hoods and gloves. At such low temperatures, if you touch the car with bare hands, your skin would "weld" to the metal!

Testing outdoors and in

Each prototype in the BMW 7 series was driven over 10,000 miles on all types of roads, from frozen Arctic lakes (left) to the intense heat of Death Valley in California. Indoors, vibration rigs (below) allow a lifetime of driving to be simulated in days. After testing, each car was crushed!

A SMASHING SUPERCAR

Crash testing is an essential procedure, and each test must be planned and recorded in the minutest detail. There can only be a few attempts, since each prototype costs so much money. Dummies bristling with sensors and recording equipment are strapped into the seats, to check for possible injury. Recording instruments are also attached to the car. A steel tow cable pulls the car into the crash wall at a controlled speed. High-speed photography (3,000 pictures per second) records the impact.

Robots and frames

The chassis is the supporting structure for the bodywork. It also provides a "safety cage" in the event of accidents. Jigs align the chassis parts and computer-controlled industrial robots weld them together. Great accuracy enables the fittings and body panels to be positioned and exactly adjusted. The robot's control program can be altered to build other models.

Coats of paint

Complete immersion in rust-resistant primer is the answer for all-over protection. Accurately positioned holes are made to allow the paint to reach all areas, and these are later filled. When later coats of paint are put on, electrostatic dusters rotating at high speed ensure that no dust is present to spoil the shiny finish. Automated sprays use economical amounts of paint.

Wires and cables

More than 1,500 yards of color-coded electrical wires and cables must be installed, in positions determined in the prototypes. They connect the battery; electrical equipment and control systems. A robot arm helps assembly workers to position the heavy, lead-filled battery.

On the line

The production line is a coordinated sequence of operations. At each stage, quality control is carried out to ensure that the car is put together perfectly.

Look – no doors

After painting, the doors are removed. This "doorless assembly" allows workers to move freely in the car's interior as they position seats and fittings. At this stage, craftspeople examine every detail to ensure the quality and comfort.

PRODUCTION

Many standard cars are built almost entirely by robots. But the manufacture of a Supercar requires the skills of craftspeople to iron out any small blemishes, as well as robots for routine tasks. This gives it the very best finish as it moves automatically from stage to stage.

The buyer of a Supercar will expect to be given a wide range of options, for equipment fitted inside the car as well as the more usual choices of engine size and body color. Details of each customer's exact requirements are fed into a computer. When the time comes for that car to be built, the computerized warehouse ensures that the necessary parts are delivered to the right place on the production line, at the correct time. Because parts are obtained from a variety of suppliers, the production

Engine and suspension

Construction of the engine and gearbox takes place on another production line at the same time as the body. The two are now "married" together, with human guidance, and the wheels and suspension are fitted. Finishing touches are now added.

Glass in the windows

The doors reappear at both sides of the car (to avoid unnecessary handling) and are fitted to the body. The correct tool is always at hand, suspended from an overhead girder. Glass is now fitted in the windows.

system must ensure that those parts are delivered in good time. A standby supplier is arranged, to step in if there are problems. The whole operation is a masterpiece of logical planning. Engineers and planners use yet more computer programs to make sure that, whatever happens, production can continue.

ON THE ROAD

And so, after years of research and development, the Supercar is finally on the road. But the story does not end here. Now it must be maintained in peak condition for its working life. It has to be serviced when required, to avoid any possibility of breakdowns and the inconvenience these bring to the owner.

As more durable (long-lasting) materials are developed, and lubrication systems become more efficient, so the intervals between servicing become longer. On-board computers advise of faults as and when they occur, and in time to avoid complete failure. So regular servicing, with the exception of routine oil changes, is becoming a thing of the past.

When the car does need attention, it no longer requires hours of investigation. As long ago as the 1960s, some Volkswagen cars were fitted with a plug-in terminal so that engine performance could be monitored. Today's Supercar is plugged into a servicing computer that reads all the information stored in the on-board computer. It then provides a printout of points needing attention.

Computer meets computer
The on-board computer is linked to the servicing computer by a special connector (right). A printout of the information stored on-board is then made. The servicing computer has two functions. In static mode it identifies problems and parts in need of replacement. In dynamic mode (below) it "tests" the car, making parts move to check that they are working correctly.

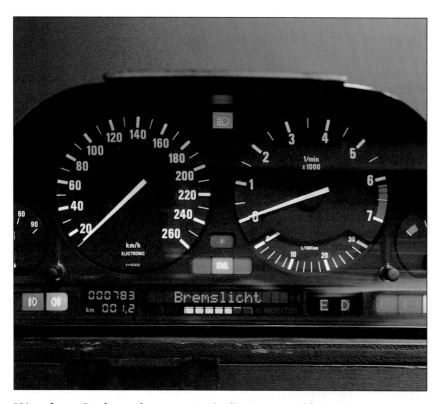

Warning: On-board computer indicates a malfunction.

```
900 DEFECT SURVEY

999 DEFECT MEMORY
    CANCEL



SELECT: NUMBER AND ⊕

BACK ↑
  R
```

Computer printout

The printout gives the servicing mechanic a list of options about which parts to investigate. Initially the choice is betwen making a fault survey or erasing the on-board memory (this is done at the end of each service).

```
       CONTROL UNIT SURVEY
*01-DIGITAL MOTOR ELECTR.       DME
*02-CENTR. BODY ELECTR.         ZKE
*03-CLUSTER/CHECK CONTROL       K/CC
*04-AUTOM. AIR COND.            IHKA
 05-HEATER                      IHR
*06-ON-BOARD COMPUTER           BC
*07-EH TRANSMISSION             AEGS
 08-BURGLAR ALARM               DWA
*09-SEAT/MIRROR MEMORY          SPM/SM
 10-AIRBAG                      AB
  *-BRIEF TESTING

    SYSTEM SELECTION: PUT IN
    NUMBER AND ⊕-BUTTON
    R
```

Control unit survey

Having selected the fault survey, a list of the various control units is printed out. This has code numbers and abbreviations. An asterisk (*) against the number shows that the control unit is actually fitted to this car. The system required is chosen by keying in its code number, in this case 07.

```
07 AEGS
     CONTROL UNIT IDENTIFICATION

BMW PART NUMBER          1 218 ...
SOFTWARE NUMBER          00.
BOSCH PART NUMBER        0 ... 002 010
SOFTWARE NUMBER          1 267 355 390
ZF PART NUMBER           1A 44 929 066
CODING                   00



CONTINUE ↓              BACK ↑
```

Unit identification

Code 07 tests the electro-hydraulic transmission system. The part number of the control unit is displayed together with the part numbers of suppliers. If the control unit should need replacing, those are the part numbers to ask for at the stores.

```
07 AEGS

100 STATIC CALLING
200 DYNAMIC CALLING
300 COMPONENT OPERATION
900 DEFECT SURVEY -
    PRINT OUT INFORMATION WITH R
999 CANCEL DEFECT MEMORY
  - CARRY OUT AFTER ELIMINATION
    OF DEFECTS!

 #  NOTES

SELECT: NUMBER AND ⊕
                       BACK ↑
  R
```

Test procedure

Another menu (list of options) now appears for selecting the type of test procedure. Code 100 selects static testing. This instructs the computer to check any faults that have been recorded by the on-board computer since the last service, and print out a list (code 900). Code 200 selects dynamic testing, making the car do the work. The code 300, component operation, puts it into action, in this case by changing gear.

```
       CONTROL UNIT SURVEY
*01-DIGITAL MOTOR ELECTR.       DME
*03-CLUSTER/CHECK-CONTROL       K/CC
*06-ON-BOARD COMPUTER           BC
*07-EH TRANSMISSION             AEGS
 08-BURGLAR ALARM               DWA
 11-EL ENGINE POWER CONTR.      EML
 12-DIGITAL DIESEL ELECTR.      DDE
 21-IR SYSTEM                   IRS

  *-BRIEF TESTING

    SELECT SYSTEM: INPUT
    OF NUMBER AND ⊕ BUTTON
    R  BRIEF TEST FINISHED
```

IN THE MARKETPLACE

Few car manufacturers are in business for fun. Pressure is on the engineers and designers to come up with a car that is more desirable than others in its class, and which will therefore take a "lion's share" of the market. In the case of standard models, low cost is a major selling point, along with economy and reliability. But in the case of the Supercars, "ultimate" is the key word. This might apply to luxury, performance, or simply the status of owning one.

A Supercar is often the flagship of its line. If it can out-perform its rivals, then people may be tempted to buy more standard models by the same manufacturer. This is one reason why car makers invest such enormous sums of money in Supercar development, even though they may only sell a few hundred top-of-the-line models. To justify this investment, a very large number of cars must eventually be sold throughout the line.

SPINNING OFF THE TECHNOLOGY

Much of the technology in a newly-developed car can be re-used for upgrading an existing model. This helps to spread the costs. For example, the third-generation BMW 5 series, launched in 1988 (right), owes much to its bigger sister. The front and rear suspension systems, the speed-related power-assisted steering and the upgraded engines were all inherited from the 7 series. So were the air conditioning, automatic seatbelt height adjustment – and, of course, the on-board computers!

Supercars for Super-buyers
Three other Supercars of today are the Jaguar XJ6, the Mercedes-Benz S Class, and the Lincoln Continental (a "Super-limo"). Each has favorable points. The Jaguar may not be exceptionally high-tech, but it has a timeless quality (and lower price). The Mercedes has much in common technically with the BMW but even so there is a different appeal. The Lincoln remains "typically American," but also has up-to-date systems such as active suspension and anti-lock braking. The automotive press puts each new Supercar under the microscope, but in the end it is the customer who decides.

Jaguar XJ6

Mercedes-Benz S Class

Lincoln Continental

THE YOUNG ENGINEER

Cars have been traveling on roads for more than a century. In the beginning, the machinery was uncomplicated and the driver had to do most of the work. Today, the complex control systems of a Supercar handle dozens of jobs every second. Yet they still use many simple engineering principles. Try the projects shown here, which demonstrate some of the basic scientific principles involved in designing and driving a car.

That streamlined shape

A car's shape is important for two main reasons. One: to give a low wind resistance (a low *drag coefficient*) and so increase efficiency. Two: to keep the car in firm (and so safe) contact with the road, by shaping it so that the air passing over the car presses it downward. You can see the effect of wind resistance in the drawings below. The sleek-shaped car (1) has a low drag coefficient and the air passes smoothly over it. If it were placed in a box (2), this would disturb the airflow (produce turbulence) and slow it down. Try a simple project to show this, by resting one end of a wooden board on books to give a gentle slope. Place a fan (or hold a hairdryer) at the lower end, to blow up the slope. Let a toy car roll down, and measure the time it takes to travel from top to bottom (3). Now fix a small box over the car – making sure it does not touch the board and produce friction – and repeat the experiment (4). The "box-car" should take longer to reach the bottom because of extra wind resistance (page 6).

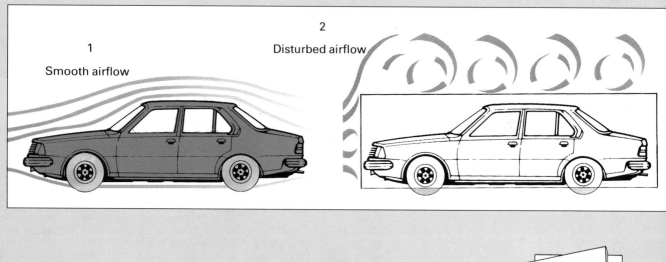

1 Smooth airflow

2 Disturbed airflow

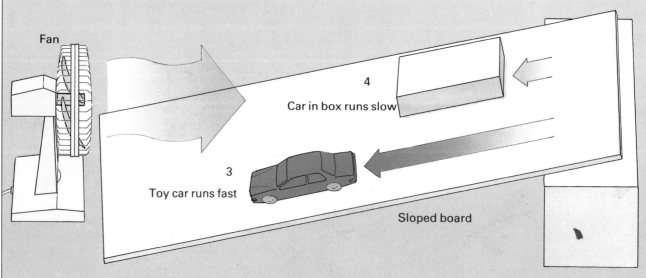

Fan

4 Car in box runs slow

3 Toy car runs fast

Sloped board

A lower design

To prevent a car from tipping over when cornering at speed, the center of gravity (center of mass) must be low (1). Otherwise the centrifugal (outward) force makes it tilt up and over the outer wheels (2). Lay a rectangular block of wood flat on a table (3). It has a low center of gravity (shown by the dot) in this position. Prevent it from sliding sideways and try to tip it up. It's not easy! Now stand the block on its side (4). With the center of gravity higher, it tips much more easily (page 6).

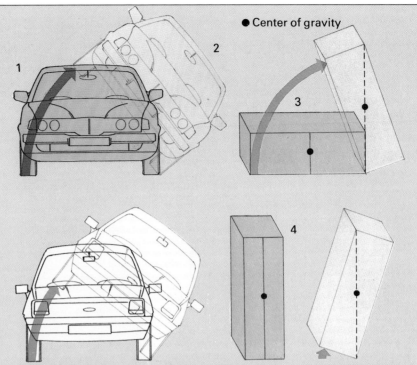

● Center of gravity

Friction: friend and foe

A low profile tire (1) has a large contact patch (area in contact with the road) and grips better than a narrow tire (2). Place the toy car inside a large matchbox and slide it down a steeply-sloping wooden board (3). Measure the time from top to bottom. Now repeat the test run with the car inside a much smaller matchbox (4). It should reach the bottom more quickly. The larger box has a greater contact area so that there is more friction to prevent slipping (page 20). However, friction can be the engineer's enemy. A large amount of engine power is used to overcome friction where two parts move against each other, such as pistons inside cylinders and shafts in their casings. In both cases the area of contact is kept to a minimum with piston rings or ball bearings. Lubrication with oil or grease reduces friction (page 19).

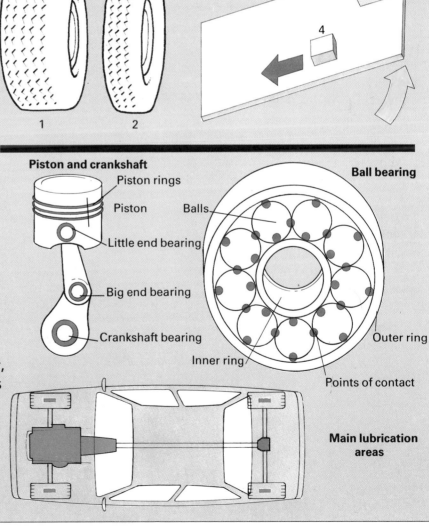

Piston and crankshaft

Piston rings

Piston

Little end bearing

Big end bearing

Crankshaft bearing

Ball bearing

Balls

Outer ring

Inner ring

Points of contact

Main lubrication areas

CARS COMPARED

The car industry is a world of changing fortunes. The success of a particular model depends not only on its individual appeal but also on the appeal of its rivals from other manufacturers. So designers and engineers are always fully occupied in the constant search for better economy, safety, performance, style – and something new that no other car can offer. Active suspension and anti-lock braking are relatively new technologies, and four-wheel steering is also being developed. By the time these become commonplace, something else will be emerging from the research engineer's workshop. Automatic navigation systems are already being tested, and more and more electronics are taking routine tasks away from the driver and mechanic.

What is a "cc"?

The "cc" of car engine sizes stands for *cubic centimeter*. It is a measure of the amount of air pushed aside when the piston makes its complete travel in the cylinder – the swept volume. In a 4-cylinder car with an engine size of 4,000 cc, each piston sweeps aside 1,000 cc of air during its cycle (page 11). Since 1,000 cc = 1 liter, a 4,000 cc car is also a 4 liter car.

FROM RACE TRACK TO DRIVEWAY

Formula 1 racing car:	Honda-engined Lotus
Maximum speed	210 mph
Acceleration 0-60 mph	2.8 seconds
Fuel consumption	4 mpg
Engine size	1500cc V-6
GT (Le Mans) sports car:	**Porsche 917**
Maximum speed	250 mph
Acceleration 0-60 mphh	3.8 seconds
Fuel consumption	7 mpg
Engine size	5000 cc flat-12
Production sports car:	**Lamborghini Countach**
Maximum speed	179 mph
Acceleration 0-60 mph	4.9 seconds
Fuel consumption	19 mpg
Engine size	5167 cc V-12
Supercar production saloon:	**BMW 750**
Maximum speed	156 mph
Acceleration 0-60 mph	7.4 seconds
Fuel consumption	25 mpg
Engine size	4988 cc V-12
Family hatchback:	**Citroen 19BX**
Maximum speed	114 mph
Acceleration 0-60 mph	10.1 seconds
Fuel consumption	37 mpg
Engine size	1905 cc inline-4
Economy small-car:	**Austin Mini**
Maximum speed	84 mph
Acceleration 0-60 mph	19.7 seconds
Fuel consumption	44 mpg
Engine size	998 cc inline-4

FASTEST

Land speed records for wheel-driven cars:
690 mph Bluebird (turbine engined)
673 mph Goldenrod (piston engined)

CONVERSION FACTORS

Speed

1 mph (mile per hour) = 1.6 km/h (kilometers per hour). As a rough guide, 50 mph = 80 km/h, 70 mph = 110 km/h, and 100 mph = 160 km/h.

Fuel

1 gallon = 3.8 liters. So a car that has a 15-gallon tank holds about 57 liters. 1 liter = 0.26 gallons, and a 50-liter tank takes about 13 gallons.

Economy

1 mpg (mile per gallon) = 278 l/100 km (liters per 100 km). So 20 mpg = 14 l/100 km, and 50 l/100 km = 5.5 mpg. These measures are opposites – a high mpg or a low l/100 km means good fuel economy.

GLOSSARY

Active suspension A computer-controlled system that keeps the car body level by adjusting the suspension at each wheel (see also Suspension).

Aerodynamics The shape of a car in relation to how the air flows past it. Good aerodynamics give a low drag coefficient.

Air bag A safety device mounted on the steering wheel, which inflates in the event of a collision to prevent chest injuries to the driver.

Anti-lock braking system (ABS) A computer-controlled system for maximum braking efficiency. It alternately releases and applies brake pressure to individual wheels to prevent wheel lock and skidding, no matter how hard the driver presses the brake pedal.

Automatic transmission Changing the engine speed relative to the road speed automatically, by means of gears.

Catalytic converter Part of an exhaust system that converts polluting exhaust gases to harmless ones when they pass over the hot metals inside it.

Center of gravity The imaginary point in any object at which the weight is centered.

Computer management A computer system that monitors engine performance and makes adjustments to maintain peak efficiency.

Computer-aided design A computer system that, among other things, enables an engineer to enter design information and see what effect it will have on the car.

Disk brakes A steel disk attached to the car wheel which is gripped between stationary pads when the brake pedal is pushed.

Fuel injection A method of supplying fuel to the engine cylinders by injecting accurately controlled doses.

Hydraulic brakes A system of applying the brakes in which the pressure of the foot on the brake pedal is transmitted by an oily liquid in pipes to the brakes.

Power-assisted steering A method of reducing the effort needed to turn the steering wheel, using oil pressurized by the engine.

Prototype One of the first of a new design of car, which is used for testing before the car goes into full production.

Safety cage A reinforced safety structure around the passenger compartment to reduce injury in a collision.

Spark plug Two insulated metal prongs across which a spark leaps when a high voltage is fed to one of them. The spark ignites the fuel/air mixture in the cylinder.

Supercar A high performance, technically advanced luxury car with many refinements for the comfort and safety of the driver and passengers.

Suspension The connecting system between the wheels and the body, which smooths out bumps and hollows in the road. It determines the stability of the car (see also Active suspension).

Transmission The system of gears and shafts that transmits the turning of the engine to the wheels.

Turbocharger A specially-shaped compressor fan (turbine), operated by the exhaust gases, which forces air into the engine to improve performance.

INDEX

Photographic Credits:
Cover and pages 6 (all), 7 (all), 14 (all), 15 (all), 16, 17, 18 (all), 19 (all), 20 (all), 21 (all), 22 (all), 23 (all), 24, 25 and 27: BMW AG Germany; page 10: Vanessa Bailey; page 11: Ford Motor Co.; page 26 (left): Autocar/Haymarket Publishing; page 26: Quadrant Picture Library.